EVOLUTION

EVOLUTION

Written by **Daniel Loxton**

Illustrated by **Daniel Loxton**
with **Jim W.W. Smith**

Kids Can Press

DEDICATION

For my brilliant wife, Cheryl Hebert, and for my good friend Pat Linse.
You created this project, both of you, with your sacrifice and support.

Credits

Additional photography by David Patton, Jason Loxton and Julie Roberts
Preliminary line art and 3-D modeling by Jim W.W. Smith
Science Consultant: Dr. Donald Prothero, Lecturer in Geobiology,
California Institute of Technology, and Professor of Geology, Occidental College

Text and illustrations © 2010 Daniel Loxton

Based on *Junior Skeptic* material originally published within *Skeptic* magazine — www.skeptic.com.
Funding for *Junior Skeptic* "Evolution" material provided by Pat Linse. *Junior Skeptic* created by Pat
Linse. *Junior Skeptic* "Evolution" illustrations created by Daniel Loxton with Jim W. W. Smith.

Kids Can Press gratefully acknowledges the financial support of the
Government of Ontario, through the Ontario Media Development Corporation;
the Ontario Arts Council; the Canada Council for the Arts; and the Government of
Canada, through the CBF, for our publishing activity.

Published in Canada and the U.S. by Kids Can Press Ltd.
25 Dockside Drive, Toronto, ON M5A 0B5

Kids Can Press is a Corus Entertainment Inc. company

www.kidscanpress.com

Edited by Valerie Wyatt
Designed by Julia Naimska

Printed and bound in Malaysia in 11/2016 by Tien Wah Press (Pte.) Ltd.

CM 10 0 9 8 7 6

Library and Archives Canada Cataloguing in Publication

Loxton, Daniel, 1975--
Evolution : how we and all living things came to be / written and
illustrated by Daniel Loxton.

Includes index.
ISBN 978-1-55453-430-2 (bound)

1. Evolution (Biology)—Juvenile literature. I. Title.

QH367.1.L69 2010   j576.8   C2009-903365-8

CONTENTS

PART 1
WHAT *IS* EVOLUTION?

Evolution is nothing less than the amazing story of life on Earth — an epic tale that has taken billions of years to unfold.

During most of its long history, Earth was a planet so alien you wouldn't recognize it. There was an ancient time when batlike reptile pterosaurs soared high above a world ruled by dinosaurs. Hundreds of millions of years before that, bizarre tentacled ocean creatures battled under the seas, while the land remained barren of plant and animal life. Long before *that,* for more than three billion years, the only life-forms were simple one-celled things you'd need a microscope to see.

Earth has been home to an astonishingly different mix of living things at every point in its long history. Why has the living world changed so often and so much? How did these changes happen?

New kinds of living things develop from older forms of life through a process called evolution. The force behind the teeming diversity of life on Earth, evolution is the most important idea in all of biology. It is the process that created the terrible teeth of *Tyrannosaurus rex* and the delicate beauty of a rose petal. Evolution is the engine that generates new diseases — and understanding evolution helps us fight those diseases.

About 150 years ago, a British scientist named Charles Darwin revealed the solution to the mystery of evolution. Darwin's amazing breakthrough was made possible by the work of other scientists, who paved the way with their important discoveries about the history of life on Earth …

CLUES TO THE PAST

One breakthrough that helped set the stage for Darwin's theory of evolution was the discovery that Earth was once home to animals that no longer exist.

For hundreds of years, many people believed that all creatures were created at the same time, and that all of them were still around. Neither of these ideas turned out to be true.

For example, a mammoth may look like a modern elephant, but it isn't one. Scientist Georges Cuvier proved that in the 1790s, when he compared fossil mammoths with elephants alive today. Mammoths were not only different from elephants — they had "gone extinct." They had died out and vanished from the Earth.

The idea that some animals had become extinct was confirmed when people found strange fossils totally unlike any living animals. One fossil hunter was a young English girl named Mary Anning. Around 1810, she discovered the first complete specimen of an extinct ichthyosaur — a reptile with a sharklike body streamlined for life in the sea.

Anning went on to find other important fossils. She was one of the great fossil hunters of all time.

The fossils discovered by Anning and others were a real shock to people. During very ancient times, Earth was home to many kinds of animals that had since gone extinct. Fossils provided rock solid evidence that life was different in the past.

But how far in the past? And what sorts of changes had occurred in living things during Earth's long history?

Ichthyosaurs were reptiles that evolved shark-shaped bodies. They ruled the sea for 150 million years, during the age of the dinosaurs.

An ichthyosaur fossil

DEEP TIME

The birth of modern geology (the study of the rocks that make up Earth's crust) supplied more pieces of the evolutionary puzzle.

In the 1800s, geologists realized that the layers in the rocks are a record of time. Most rock is slowly made from mud that settles and hardens or from lava flowing out of a volcano. Because each new layer of mud or lava gets deposited on top of older layers, a stack of layered rocks is a record of Earth's past. The farther down the stack you go, the older the rocks.

Two things soon became obvious. First, the rock record was very thick, with many miles of layers. Second, each layer of rock in the stack contained a group of fossils that no other layer had. One layer of rock = one collection of fossils = one period of time.

As geologists studied the rock layers, they realized that the further back in time you went, the less familiar the animals became. The fossils in the most recent rocks looked very similar to living animals. But fossils in the bottom layers looked hardly anything like the animals we know.

Almost all the animals in older rocks were extinct. Ammonites (marine creatures with shells), dinosaurs, mammoths, all sorts of weird creatures — all gone. Even weirder, the further back you went, the simpler life seemed to get. But what did this all mean?

It took a few million years for rushing river waters to carve out the Grand Canyon. But it took many hundreds of millions of years to lay down the many layers of rock the canyon cuts through.

ENTER CHARLES DARWIN

The clues were there, but no one had yet figured out what they meant. Then, in 1831, a young Englishman named Charles Darwin set out on a sailing ship called the *Beagle* — a voyage that would eventually lead him to solve the mystery of evolution.

A medical school dropout, Darwin was a rich kid with a passion for the natural world. It was his interest in science that led him to volunteer aboard the *Beagle*, which was on a map-making mission around the globe.

Darwin's job was to keep the captain company at dinner and to collect plant and animal specimens at the places they stopped.

While on the isolated Galápagos Islands (a chain of volcanic islands off the coast of South America), Darwin collected tortoises and birds. He took specimens from several of the islands. Later, in England, a bird expert noticed something remarkable — although the birds looked different, they were actually all finches.

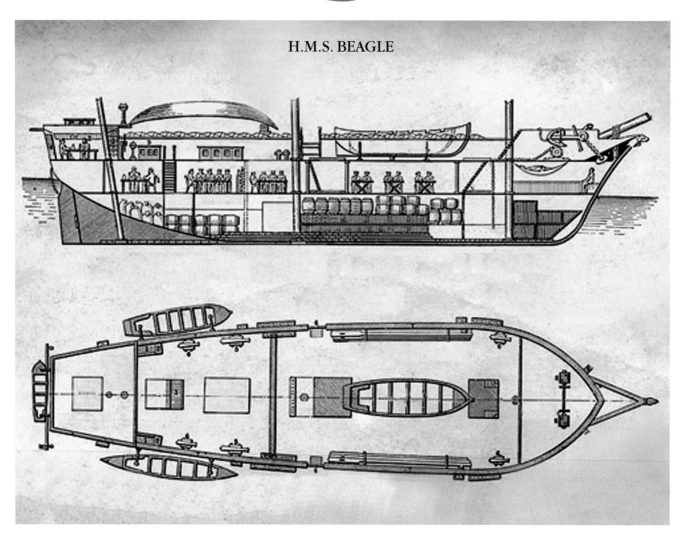

H.M.S. BEAGLE

Darwin came up with a theory to explain why the finches looked so different from one island to another. He theorized that long ago, mainland finches had been blown to the islands. Once there, they developed different adaptations to take advantage of the different foods available to them. On one island, the finches had large beaks for cracking tough seeds. On another, they had long thin beaks for catching insects and so on.

But if that was true — if one species could turn into several new species — how did it happen?

Finches' beaks are adapted to the different foods available on various Galápagos Islands.

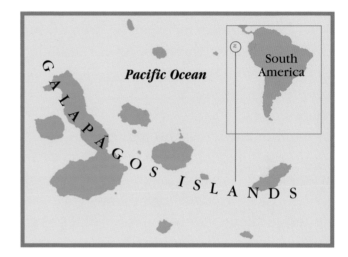

Pacific Ocean

GALÁPAGOS ISLANDS

South America

"What exactly is a species?"

A species is a group of living things that can reproduce with one another, but not with other life-forms. Cobras can breed only with cobras, giraffes with giraffes and ivory-billed woodpeckers with other ivory-billed wood-peckers. (Try breeding a shark and a poodle and you're going to be out of luck.)

For most animals and plants, this is the most useful definition of species. But this definition doesn't work for some life-forms — especially microscopic ones. Some of these life-forms don't breed together at all. Instead, they reproduce by splitting into two.

CLUES IN THE BARNYARD

To solve the mystery of evolutionary change, Darwin looked for clues in an unlikely place — the barnyard. In Darwin's time, raising pigeons was a popular hobby. There were many specialized breeds, each fancier than the last. Some pigeons were bred for outlandish air sacs on their chests or fantails like miniature peacocks or huge fluffy feathered feet. Breeding led to a wide variety of behaviors, colors, patterns, beak shapes, sizes — you name it.

Darwin knew that this tremendous variety arose from breeding just one species of wild pigeon. Breeders looked for differences in their pigeons and allowed birds with desirable features to have more babies. They might select the pigeons with the fluffiest feet or the largest tails to breed or whatever trait (variation) the breeder preferred.

Over many generations, people continued this process of selecting certain traits, which eventually led to new breeds. Darwin saw that evolution was happening in farmyards every day through this selection process.

All farm animals evolved into their current form because people selected the traits that were most useful to them and continue to do so today. Modern cows have been bred to produce more

As a way to test his ideas about selection, Darwin spent years breeding and studying pigeons.

milk, and pigs more meat. Modern domestic sheep hardly resemble their wild ancestors, which had hair instead of wool. Plant crops were also bred from very different wild ancestors. Grains like rice, oats and wheat are all modified forms of grasses.

If the selection process was taking place on farms, could it also be happening naturally in the wild, Darwin wondered?

PIGEON BREEDING SPEEDED UP

Breed these two wild pigeons and you might get …

… a pigeon with feathered feet. Breed it with another feather-footed pigeon and you might get …

… a pigeon with super feathery feet. Over time and many generations, this trait could be reinforced over and over again.

THE POPULATION PUZZLE

Darwin realized something very important. In the wild, living things produce far more offspring than can possibly survive. Some plants, for example, produce millions of seeds — far more than they need to replace themselves. Even animals that reproduce slowly, such as elephants, produce too many offspring. If all those offspring survived, the planet would be overrun.

Luckily for us, that doesn't happen. Instead, populations are kept under control by factors such as predators, food and climate.

Darwin saw that all living things must struggle to survive, and he wondered why some survived this struggle while others didn't. What made some living things better able to survive than others?

This question was Darwin's breakthrough — and his answer changed the face of science forever.

Start with a male and female rabbit and you'll soon be overrun with rabbits.

DARWIN'S BIG IDEA

Finally, Darwin put all the pieces together. He solved the ultimate scientific mystery: how nature produces new species of living things.

Darwin knew that new traits popped up from time to time in the wild. Some of these variations were helpful in the struggle to survive, but others made survival harder.

If a natural variation gave a plant or animal an advantage, that plant or animal would be more likely to survive to have offspring. And, as Darwin knew from breeding pigeons, those individuals would also pass on their useful traits to their offspring. This meant the next generation would also have an advantage in the struggle to survive — and useful variations could add up over many generations.

Catch that? Let's look at it one more time: Individuals born with a trait that gives them an advantage have a better chance of surviving and reproducing.

On the other hand, Darwin wrote, individuals born with bad variations would be at a disadvantage and would be much less likely to survive and reproduce. And then he summed up his theory: "This preservation of favorable variations and the rejection of injurious variations, I call Natural Selection."

This dinosaur inherited large size and a long neck from its parents and their ancestors. These useful traits gave these animals advantages in the struggle to survive.

That was it — Darwin's Big Idea. It's so simple, you could fit it on a T-shirt. In short, Darwin's Theory of Natural Selection says:

1. All creatures struggle to survive and reproduce, but many fail.
2. Creatures that happen to be born with an advantageous trait are the most likely to reproduce.
3. Parents pass on their advantageous traits to their offspring.

From there, all it takes is time!

WORDS OF CAUTION

As you read on, you'll read about how evolution does this or evolution does that. But, in fact, evolution doesn't "do" anything — it's a process by which things happen. Saying "evolution does this or that" is just a shortcut, a way to compare things in the world with familiar human activities. There's no intelligence — no brain — behind evolution that is running things. Instead, evolution is a process that happens naturally and unthinkingly, like the weather.

GREAT MINDS THINK ALIKE

Darwin knew that his theory of evolution would be controversial. Some people would find the idea that new species arose from old ones hard to believe. Others would think natural selection was too simple an idea to explain the diversity of life. Finally, some people would dislike Darwin's theory for religious reasons — they believed that a supreme being created the variety of plants and animals, not nature. For many years, Darwin continued to work on his ideas in secret.

Then, unexpectedly, another English naturalist discovered natural selection on his own. The young Alfred Russel Wallace noticed the same connections between animals isolated on separate islands that Darwin had discovered many years before.

Their ideas were presented together to a prestigious scientific society in 1858, and the two men shared credit for the discovery.

HOW CHANGE HAPPENS

Darwin noticed that plants and animals had traits that made them more or less likely to survive. He also knew that parents could pass their traits on to their offspring. But how did new traits come about? And how were traits passed on to the next generation? In Darwin's time, 150 years ago, people could only guess. Today, we know that it's all in the genes.

Inside every cell of every living thing (including you) is a long, complicated chainlike molecule called DNA. It contains the chemically coded instructions — called "genes" — for growing that living thing. Your genes instruct your cells to divide in a way that gives you certain traits. For example, you might have genes for curly hair or straight, blue eyes or brown and so on — everything that makes you who you are.

Many people describe this genetic code as being like a blueprint. After all, DNA does include instructions for building something. But biologist Richard Dawkins thinks DNA is more like a recipe. A blueprint describes a thing, but a recipe describes a process for making a thing. Like a cake recipe, DNA is a set of instructions for a process of development. If those instructions are followed, a cell can divide over and over and eventually grow into a plant or animal or other living thing.

This difference between blueprints and recipes is important for understanding evolution. If living things had blueprints, one part could be moved or redesigned or substituted without much affecting the whole organism. But suppose you misread a recipe and accidentally changed the cooking time or substituted salt for sugar. You would change the entire cake.

So, DNA is a lot like a recipe for growing a living thing. And change happens when there is an error, called a mutation, in those genetic instructions.

We're All Mutants

You are a result of mutations — and so is every other living thing.

A mutation is an accidental, permanent change in the genetic instructions for making a living thing. Because mutations are random changes, they can have either harmful or helpful effects. For example, some women have a mutation that makes them much more likely to get breast cancer. Some other people have mutations that protect them from diseases such as River Blindness, which, as its name suggests, can cause blindness.

A mutation can have a big or small impact or no detectable impact at all. It all depends on which DNA instructions are changed, and how big those changes are.

Some genetic instructions are so important that any change will be bad. For example, all animals share a "master gene" for growing eyes. Changes to that gene result in deformed eyes — or no eyes at all.

Genetic instructions are delicately balanced, so sudden large changes are likely to cause problems. On the other hand, small mutations have a reasonable chance of being neutral (not harmful) and may even be helpful. For example, many people carry the harmless mutation that causes blue eyes. Another mutation makes a few fortunate people immune to the virus that causes AIDS.

When you're talking about mutations, the smaller the better. But, as time passes, many small changes can add up to big differences.

"Mutants" in the movies can have superhuman body parts and abilities or super-bad personalities and looks. These fantastic exaggerations are inspired by the real biological idea of "mutation," or random genetic change.

19

MUTATIONS + TIME = EVOLUTION

Have you played the game "telephone"? One player whispers a sentence to the person beside them, who whispers it to the next person. As the message is passed along, changes creep in. Each change is usually small — say, one word accidentally switched for another. But those changes add up, because the changes become part of the message. And the longer the chain of players, the more changes sneak in. By the time the last person repeats the message out loud, it barely resembles the original sentence.

The same is true of the DNA "message" — small mutations that get passed down through generations of living things can result in big changes over time.

And evolution does take time. Lots of it. The story of evolution has unfolded over billions of years. Evolution happens S-L-O-W-L-Y. It usually takes thousands of years for new species of animals to evolve — sometimes millions of years.

"Can we ever see evolution happening?"

Yes. Occasionally, we *can* watch evolution in action. Take the peppered moth, which is found in many parts of England. Most of these insects were light colored with dark pepperlike speckles, while a rare few were dark all over. The common peppered pattern was good camouflage against the light-colored bark and lichens on the trees where the moths liked to rest. The less common darker moths were easier for birds to spot and gobble up.

That was true until the Industrial Revolution, which started in the late 1700s. As people began to burn more coal to power new factories, coal smoke spread over the countryside. It killed the light-colored lichens and blackened the trees with soot. When the moths' habitat darkened, the light peppered pattern stopped being good camouflage. Instead, the peppered moths now stood out more than the dark moths, making them easy prey for hungry birds.

Suddenly, dark moths had a better chance of surviving and breeding. The dark coloring stopped being a problem and became an advantage. This advantage was passed along to new generations.

Within a hundred years, almost all the moths were dark colored. A change in the environment led to a physical adaptation in the moths. That's natural selection and evolution in action!

Moths with this speckled pattern were most common because they had better camouflage …

… until coal pollution altered their environment. Then the previously rare darker moths had the advantage, and soon became the most common type.

BIG CHANGES = NEW SPECIES

Over time, small mutations can lead to big changes in plants and animals — so big that one species can even split into two.

How? Let's imagine a species of zebra-like animal (we'll call them Zooks) that lives in a particular valley. Healthy male and female Zooks can breed because they are members of the same species and so are genetically compatible.

But what if some Zooks moved into a nearby but isolated valley where tough shrubs grew instead of the sweet grasses of the original valley? As the generations go by, the two populations are put under different natural selection pressures. For example, an ability to digest grasses would be a big advantage in the original valley, while an ability to chew tough shrubs might be more useful in the second valley. Slowly, over many generations, genetic differences would start to build up in the Zooks of the two valleys.

Members of the same species are able to produce healthy offspring together because their genetic codes are similar and compatible.

Ugh.

Ech.

If a species splits into different isolated groups, those groups may eventually accumulate so many genetic changes that it becomes impossible for them to produce healthy offspring together.

Now imagine that once every few generations, a Zook from one valley wanders into the other valley and gets stuck there. For many generations, such wandering Zooks can still find mates easily enough because the Zooks in both valleys are the same species.

But, as the generations go by and genetic differences build up, new obstacles start to make it harder for the Zooks from the two valleys to produce healthy offspring together. For example, Zooks from one valley may evolve a unique new mating dance or a new color that is attractive only to Zooks from their own valley.

More importantly, as genetic differences increase between the Zooks of the two valleys, interbreeding becomes less possible. At first, small genetic differences may lead to rare birth defects or a smaller chance of a pregnancy occurring in the first place. After many generations, larger genetic differences may make it outright impossible for pregnancy to happen. Or the offspring from crossbreeding may be sterile, unable to have babies of their own.

When it becomes virtually impossible for the Zooks from one valley to breed with Zooks from the other valley, they have evolved into two distinct species.

"But have we ever actually seen a new species evolve?"

Yes, we have seen new species evolve — both in the wild and in the lab.

In one famous lab experiment, scientists divided fruit flies into two groups and fed each group a different kind of food. Over many generations, the flies adapted to the two kinds of food. Then, the scientists introduced flies from the different groups to one another and discovered that the flies from each group would breed only with other flies from the same group. One species had become two.

Something similar happened in the wild when the subway system was built in London, England, in the 1880s. Mosquitoes from the surface established breeding colonies down inside the warm tunnels. These underground mosquitoes found new food sources, and today they no longer breed with the mosquitoes from the surface. They have divided into two distinct species.

Fruit flies are great for studying evolution in the lab because they breed very quickly and easily. They're also cheap and don't take up much room. This makes it easy for scientists to breed and compare large groups of fruit flies over many generations.

23

EVOLUTION'S BODY SHOP

Hot-rodders love to make over old cars. They take an old car, fix it, repaint it, customize it and turn it into a new car.

The process of evolution does something similar. Through mutation and natural selection, nature "tinkers" with old life forms to produce new life forms. But the key concept is "tinker" — to make small improvements to something as you go along. When a new species evolves, it builds on what already exists — an accumulation of past evolutionary changes.

Hot-rod builders can lift a car or drop it, chop the roof, tint the windows and slap on some new paint — whatever they can think of to improve the car they started with. But they do not start with nothing — they start with a basic plan they've inherited from a century of car design.

Evolutionary change also builds on what was already there. We know that hundreds of millions of years ago all life was very general and simple, so all sorts of radical and bizarre new sorts of living things evolved in many different directions. This is how life got split off into its main branches (for example, fungi, plants and animals).

As time went by, the branches of life got more specialized and refined, and important design elements got somewhat "locked in."

Consider wheels on cars. A hot-rodder can swap in fat tires or skinny tires, different rims and treads and so on — but the car will still have four wheels. That's because automobile designers long ago decided on a four-wheeled design. It's possible to make perfectly good three-wheeled or six-wheeled vehicles, but it's better to build them from the ground up rather than try to modify a regular four-wheeler. To do that, you'd have to completely rebuild every detail of the car, starting with the frame.

In living things, it's much the same. Take legs, for example. As earthworms, starfish and centipedes show us, you can build a perfectly good animal with almost any number of legs — or no legs. But many modern land animals were locked into a four-legged design very early on, way back when their fishy ancestors were first emerging onto dry land. (Birds and bats and humans have modified front legs that we call "wings" or "arms," but we all still have four limbs.)

The four-legged plan can change through evolution (as it did in the case of snakes). But tried and tested basic plans tend to stay in place once they're established. For the most part, evolution just tinkers with living things. Through the process of natural selection, horses evolved from having five toes to just one, which made them larger and faster and stronger. But modern horses still have four legs, just as their ancestors did. New species are generally just updates, not radical redesigns.

This tinkering effect — lots of small and medium changes around basic common body plans inherited from common ancestors — is evolution's body shop in action.

"Why do some skeletons look so similar?"

Mammals, reptiles, birds and amphibians come in different sizes, shapes and colors, but their skeletons are put together the same way. They all have a head in the front, a tail in the back, four limbs, a skull with eye sockets and jaw, a flexible spinal column, ribs to protect their organs — and so on.

They're similar because mammals, reptiles, birds and amphibians all inherited a basic body plan from a common ancestor that lived long, long ago. Evolution has tinkered with that body plan many times, creating animals as different as mice and hummingbirds and elephants. But even the wing bones of a hummingbird are just modified versions of a land animal's leg bones.

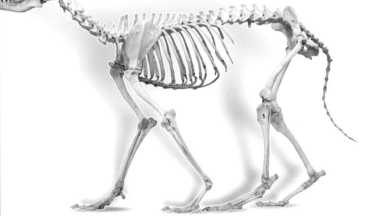

This skeleton could be almost any mammal. It looks a lot like a cat's skeleton and not much different from a sheep's. It even looks similar to a human on all fours — same bones in the same positions. But it is a wolf skeleton.

COMMON SOLUTIONS FOR COMMON PROBLEMS

The pterosaur below looks a lot like a bat or a bird, doesn't it? But this pterosaur lived 80 million years ago, long before there were bats or birds. So how did such very different animals develop with the same basic body shape and wings?

Sometimes a resemblance is a defensive disguise evolved to scare off predators. One animal may look like another animal that is fierce, tastes unpleasant or is poisonous. For

Pterosaurs
(prehistoric flying reptiles)
had body plans very similar to those
of birds and bats, even though these
three types of flying animals all evolved
independently from non-flying ancestors.

example, there are harmless moths and flies that look almost exactly like stinging wasps.

But bats and birds aren't imitating extinct pterosaurs. Their resemblance is the result of something called "convergent evolution" — the tendency for living things to evolve similar features in response to similar challenges in their environments. Birds, bats and pterosaurs each independently evolved a similar body simply because that body shape, with a pair of wings, was a good design for flying. Evolution produced other designs, too (including small gliding dinosaurs with four wings), but a two-winged, birdlike shape is the most efficient. That's why airplane designers also chose this shape.

For any task in nature, some designs are more efficient than others, and those designs tend to be favored by natural selection. To go fast underwater, the best design is a streamlined shape like a torpedo. That's why predatory fish such as sharks and tuna look like torpedoes. Even dolphins, which are descended from land animals (that's why they have lungs instead of gills), wound up evolving a torpedo body shape. The same thing happened during the age of the dinosaurs, when reptiles from dry land evolved adaptations for life in the sea. Back then, ichthyosaurs also evolved torpedo-shaped bodies. That streamlined shape works best for swimming predators.

This pattern of repeated, convergent design is common in nature. Examples are everywhere. Several groups of mammals independently evolved the same feature for catching ants: a long, sticky tongue. "Saber-toothed" predators appeared four times during Earth's long evolutionary history because their long, saberlike front teeth were great for slicing deep into the flesh of large prey animals.

The details may be different — birds, bats and pterosaurs evolved wings of similar shape, but each of their wings uses a different set of modified leg bones to get the job done. But these flying animals all evolved the same overall body shape because it works so well.

Dolphin

Shark

Ichthyosaur

The body plans of dolphins, sharks and ichthyosaurs converged on one highly efficient shape — the same shape human engineers copied for submarines.

In Australia, the extinct thylacine (right) evolved a body plan and skull structure almost identical to the wild dog (left) — but thylacines were pouched marsupials like kangaroos.

SURVIVAL OF THE FITTEST?

If there's one phrase that sums up evolution for most people, it's "survival of the fittest." Charles Darwin borrowed this phrase from someone else because it so nicely expressed what he was trying to explain about natural selection.

A mutation can be either helpful or harmful, but a living thing with a harmful mutation will be less likely to pass on that gene because its offspring will be less able to survive and reproduce. A living thing with a helpful mutation will be more likely to have offspring that can survive and reproduce, so helpful mutations tend to get passed on. In this way, the "fittest" animals (the ones with the greatest natural advantages) are the ones most likely to survive and pass on their good genes.

It's just that simple. And yet — is it ever that simple?

It's true that living things are generally well adapted to the places they live, the food they eat and so on. It is also true that some evolved traits, such as the sonar of bats, are so remarkable and sophisticated that it seems almost as if evolution can do anything.

But it can't.

Bats use sonar (or "echolocation") to tell them where things are — even in the dark. They make clicking and squeaking noises, and then interpret the echoes that bounce back to their sensitive ears.

The Limits of Evolution

Evolution is a powerful force in nature, but even it has limits.

To begin with, evolution can't make the impossible, like an animal that never needs to eat or drink or get energy from somewhere. And physics and engineering trade-offs impose other limits. For example, armored animals may evolve stronger and thicker armor, but eventually they'll reach a point where more armor would be too heavy or require too much food energy to grow. Hunting animals may evolve bigger muscles that let them run faster, but there is a point at which speed could be bone-breaking.

Another major limiting factor, as we've seen, is that evolution tinkers with what came before, through a series of small changes. Sometimes this yields surprising results. Take whales, for instance. They are descended from animals that once lived on the land and still have features inherited from these land ancestors. For example, they have lungs even though they'd be better off with gills. Having lungs means whales can actually drown, which seems ridiculous for a sea creature.

There are also limits to how good something can get. Think of an ordinary chicken egg. It might not seem like much, but it's actually a sophisticated life-support pod developed over hundreds of millions of years of evolutionary testing and revision. Since eggs are already so well made, any mutation that affects the structure of eggs is likely to be harmful. Make eggs harder, for example, and the chicks might not be able to break free when it's time to hatch. Weaken the eggs, and they might break by accident.

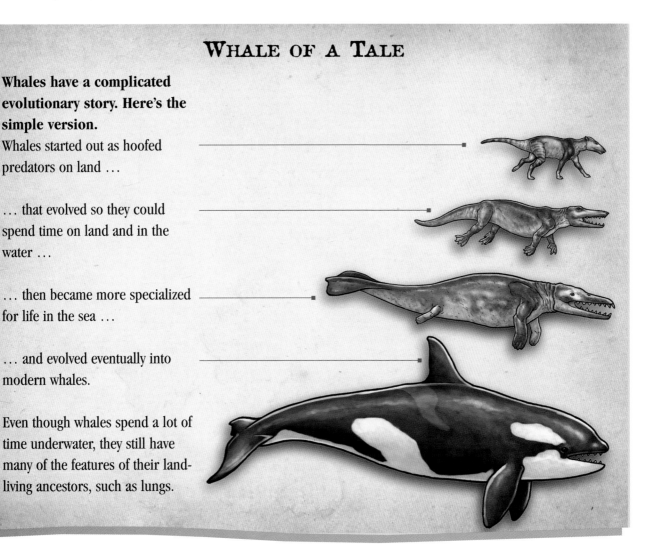

WHALE OF A TALE

Whales have a complicated evolutionary story. Here's the simple version.
Whales started out as hoofed predators on land …

… that evolved so they could spend time on land and in the water …

… then became more specialized for life in the sea …

… and evolved eventually into modern whales.

Even though whales spend a lot of time underwater, they still have many of the features of their land-living ancestors, such as lungs.

EVOLUTIONARY COMPROMISES

Evolution isn't a smooth process, and it doesn't produce perfect specimens. There are many cases in which a living thing has two needs that are contradictory. The result is often an evolutionary compromise that's good enough to meet both needs, but perfect for neither.

Biologist Richard Dawkins provides an example: Imagine that the females of one species of bird prefer males with long tails. If a male wants to find a desirable mate, he should have a nice long tail. But, long tails can be a drawback, even if female birds dig 'em. Short tails are often better for flying and escaping from predators. So, males of this species might tend, on average, to have medium tails — a compromise that is neither great nor terrible for either flirting or flying.

And there are other wrinkles to evolution. For example, changes in the genetic instructions for building an animal often have more than one effect. Just as a change to a bread recipe can change both the crust and the inside of the loaf, a genetic mutation can affect more than one part of the body. A mutation that is extremely helpful in one way can be preserved by natural selection even if it is harmful in another way.

A famous example of this is a mutation common in some groups of people from Africa. The mutation causes a terrible disease called sickle-cell anemia, which can be deadly. But this harmful mutation was preserved by natural selection because, in a weaker form, it protects people from the even more dangerous disease malaria.

Even if the short-tailed bird is faster and the long-tailed bird is handsomer, the bird with the medium tail may be the evolutionary winner.

Finally, natural selection can only favor things that are useful in the present generation, in the present form, under the current conditions. It doesn't matter if a trait would be useful far in the future, or helpful for another species in another place — traits are only selected if they're useful right now, right here.

Imagine that a hundred years from now, a deadly new disease emerges among wild sloths. And imagine that a mutation crops up today among sloths that would give their descendents complete immunity to the disease in the future. That mutation would not be favored by natural selection now, even though it might be useful later. Unless the mutation gave sloths some sort of advantage at this moment, that mutation would probably not be preserved by natural selection.

Compromise is common in nature. These prehistoric creatures evolved early adaptations for life on land (including lungs), yet they were slow and awkward when out of the water.

WHAT ABOUT US?

Did humans evolve, too? Yes! Like all living things, modern humans evolved from earlier species. We had ancestors, and they had ancestors and so on, in an unbroken chain that stretches back billions of years to the dawn of microscopic life on this planet.

During the age of the dinosaurs, our ancestors were small furry creatures that looked a bit like badgers. When the dinosaurs were wiped out, these small mammals survived, adapted to many new environments and flourished. Some evolved into a group of mammals called primates, who were adapted for life in the trees.

Eventually, some of these ancient primates began to come down from the trees to seek food on the open plains of Africa. Three million years ago, these small apelike creatures walked on two legs on the African grasslands, looking about fearfully for predators such as leopards and giant eagles. They walked upright like modern humans, but their brains were only slightly larger than modern chimpanzee brains. They were smart, but not nearly as smart as they would become.

Slowly, hominids (modern humans and our closest extinct relatives) evolved, with even bigger, more sophisticated brains. This increasing braininess gave them the ability to make and use stone and wood tools. After millions of years, hominids even learned to master fire, talk to each other, plan together and share learned skills. These brain-powered breakthroughs were something that had never occurred in nature before — and they would change the world. The tools and simple language of our ancestors would one day make human beings the dominant species on our planet.

Are humans still evolving? Yes, but in new ways, because our technologies and culture are so powerful. For example, a few thousand years ago a person with poor eyesight or weak teeth might not survive to have children. Accidents or infections might lead to an early death. Today (at least in wealthier nations), most people have access to eyeglasses and dentists.

We can't predict the ultimate impact of human technologies and ideas. No one knows what the future will bring for our species, but our brains will play an important role — just as they have for the last couple of million years of hominid evolution.

MARCH OF PROGRESS

Don't be fooled by this drawing showing evolution as a simple "March of Progress." The real story of human evolution is far more complicated, and scientists are still working on piecing it together. Although we know that the fossils of ancient human relatives *are* related, we're still working out exactly *how* they are related.

We can tell that ancient hominids are related to us by studying their skeletons, teeth and other evidence. We can also arrange the many species of extinct human relatives on a timeline: This species is older than that species and so on.

But knowing that one fossil is *older* than a related fossil doesn't tell us whether it is a *direct ancestor* of the other fossil. Think of your own family: Your father and your uncle are both closely related to you, and they're both older than you. But you're *descended* only from your father — not from your uncle.

The same is true for fossils. We can often tell that Species A was descended from either Species B or a close relative of Species B. But we can't say for sure which one.

Consider the Neanderthals. These human relatives were powerful, muscular hunters who lived in Europe until they went extinct about 30 000 years ago. Scientists are still working out whether Neanderthals are among our ancestors, or if they were a separate species *related* to our ancestors. DNA evidence now strongly suggests that Neanderthals were just an "uncle" to modern humans.

Gorillas

Chimpanzees

Bonobos

Humans

GOOD ENOUGH IS GOOD ENOUGH

I'm sorta good at catching antelopes.

I'm not too bad at getting away.

The phrase "survival of the fittest" makes it sound as though the only creatures to pass the natural selection test must be champion specimens — the Olympic athletes and Nobel Prize–winners of the natural world.

But, as you may know, most parents are neither Olympians nor geniuses!

In fact, living things don't need to be especially advanced or refined in order to pass genes to the next generation. All they have to do is just squeak by. The only measure of success in nature is simply to have offspring to continue the species.

Humans are a good example of what we might call "the survival of the adequate." We're proud of our brainpower and achievements, but as a species we're pretty so-so in many ways. In almost any habitat, we're slower, weaker and less efficient than the animals around us (including the dangerous predators).

We're not even that good at the stuff we're so famous for, such as thinking or walking upright. Humans make all sorts of thinking errors on a regular basis, some of them deadly. We forget important information, leap to false conclusions and ignore evidence. Our brains are prone to illusions and hallucinations, and emotions can easily lead us to do dangerous things. Yet, on average, we do pretty well with our brains, imperfect as they are.

And walking upright? Sure it has many advantages, including freeing our hands for carrying tools and food. But it's nowhere near a perfected system. Because our upright ancestors evolved fairly recently from creatures who walked on all fours, our bodies are only somewhat suited to walking on two legs.

Yet, here we are — good enough!

PART 2
MORE EVOLUTION QUESTIONS

Still have questions about evolution? You're not alone. Darwin revealed his theory of evolution and natural selection over 150 years ago, but nature is complex and astonishing. The details continue to puzzle curious people in every generation.

Not to worry. There are answers to the questions people commonly ask about evolution.

Could you please explain to me why I became extinct?

"How do we know that evolution happens?"

When Charles Darwin first outlined the theory of evolution 150 years ago, his evidence was based on his observations of nature and examinations of the fossilized remains of ancient animals. Since then, geologists and paleontologists (scientists who study ancient life) have confirmed and reconfirmed that life in the distant past was different from life today, that some species have gone extinct and that new species have evolved from older ones.

Today, with the help of DNA analysis, we can actually measure, rather than just observe, relatedness between living species (or recently extinct species). The DNA evidence is clear: All species are related, and all species share common ancestors. The more similar the DNA of any two species, the more recent their last common ancestor. (For example, there's hardly any genetic difference between species as closely related as chimpanzees, Neanderthals and modern humans.)

Evolution very certainly happens. But what about Darwin's explanation for how evolution happens? Does random variation (what we call "mutation" today) really produce new traits? Does natural selection really happen?

Yes, random genetic mutations can generate totally new traits in living things. Scientists routinely use random mutations to create food plants with new traits. First, they bombard thousands of seeds with radiation that causes random changes to their genetic instructions. Then they plant the seeds to see what happens. Often, the irradiated seeds don't grow or have harmful mutations. But a few have useful new traits, like resistance to disease or faster growth or more fruit. (If you've ever eaten a red grapefruit, you've probably enjoyed a fruit variety that developed from one of these random mutations.)

And, yes, natural selection is definitely a real process. For centuries we've seen that people can dramatically modify a species because breeders do it all the time. (For example, people have bred wolves to create everything from wiener dogs to greyhounds to Chihuahuas.) This selection is done by humans, but we can also observe selection happening naturally both in the lab and in nature. When viruses and bacteria develop resistance to drugs, or light-colored moths develop darker camouflage in response to sooty pollution, that's natural selection in action!

The woman on the left is a distant ancestor to the woman on the right. The modern woman inherited many traits — such as walking upright, an instinct to care for her children and using tools — from her ancestor who walked the plains of Africa three million years ago.

"If evolution really happens, where are the transitional fossils?"

A transitional fossil is a fossil that has characteristics showing it is related to two other species in the fossil record. It's an in-between fossil that demonstrates how a new plant or animal evolved from an older species into a new species. So, where are the transitional fossils?

Some people are surprised to hear it, but there are tons of them. (Literally tons — fossils are rocks, so they're awfully heavy.)

Some of the clearest sequences of transitional fossils are for ocean critters, such as ancient shellfish. Hard-shelled ocean animals fossilize easily, and there are lots of them, so they're relatively easy to find. There are fewer fossils of land animals, but scientists have still pieced together very complete fossil records — including transitional fossils — for many land animals.

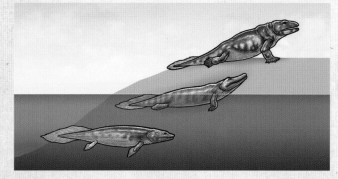

Fossils show how land animals evolved from fish.

For example, there is a detailed fossil record showing how the horse family evolved from its dog-sized ancestors. There are also excellent records that show the evolution of rhinos and elephants. (Horses, rhinos and elephants all have family trees that look more like bushes, including all sorts of really strange branches of animals that are now extinct.)

We also have fossil records for many of the most dramatic transformations in evolutionary history. For example, there is an amazingly clear record of the evolution of whales, from wolflike land mammals, to river predators shaped like giant otters, to primitive whales, to modern whales (see page 29). And there's a series of fossils illustrating how fish evolved into land animals. We even have fossils that show in detail how reptiles evolved into mammals.

But the all-time champion transitional fossil is the famous *Archaeopteryx*.

Archaeopteryx was a little feathered animal that evolved from small two-legged dinosaurs about 150 million years ago. It had the skeleton of a dinosaur, including a dinosaur's tail and teeth. But it also had major features of modern birds — it was feathered, it had wings, and it could fly.

Archaeopteryx belongs somewhere in the cluster of branching species that gave rise to modern birds, but no one is quite sure if it's a direct ancestor or just a cousin to the direct ancestor of modern birds. People who challenge the idea of evolution try to argue that *Archaeopteryx* is "just a bird" or "just a dinosaur." But *Archaeopteryx* is a champion example because it is clearly a transitional fossil, sharing the characteristics of both birds and dinosaurs. That's about as transitional as you get.

Archaeopteryx *was a small animal, about the size of a crow.*

"Isn't there a dinosaur still alive in Africa someplace? Doesn't that mean evolution didn't happen?"

People who search for Bigfoot and other legendary animals often believe in the "Mokele-mbembe." This creature is supposedly a species of four-legged, plant-eating dinosaur that believers claim is alive today in the jungles of the Congo region of Africa.

This illustration shows a Mokele-mbembe as it is typically described — a sauropod dinosaur wading in deep rivers and lakes.

As with other mysterious creatures, there are exciting tales of Mokele-mbembe encounters. But many expeditions have gone in search of this reclusive beast, and no convincing evidence has ever been found.

Some people say that if Mokele-mbembe does exist, it would spell the end of Darwin's theory. Not so. Mokele-mbembe would be another twig on the tree of evolution. It would be an example of a creature that did not become extinct and also did not change much — a so-called living fossil.

Crocodiles are such creatures. In the time of the dinosaurs, crocodiles haunted the rivers just as they do today — and they were remarkably similar to modern crocodiles. This is because crocodiles are extremely well adapted to survive, so there's much less pressure on them to change in any dramatic way.

But saying that modern crocodiles *resemble* their ancestors from millions of years ago is very different from saying they are the same *species* as their ancestors. They aren't. Like all life on Earth, "living fossils" such as crocodiles, sharks and coelacanths have evolved.

For example, their inner organs may have become bigger or smaller, their armor lighter or heavier and so on. But this evolutionary tinkering process has not radically changed them. They look pretty much the way they've always looked. The same might be said of the legendary Mokele-mbembe — if it turns out to exist, which is highly unlikely.

It's a bit like the design of hammers. All sorts of designs for hammers exist and have existed — some big, some small, some with this sort of head and some with that sort of handle. But in spite of all these little design adjustments, hammers have looked much the same ever since our ancestors first tied stones to the ends of sticks. It's no mystery: A design that works well tends to last.

Coelacanths are famous living fossils. Scientists thought all coelacanth species went extinct millions of years ago — but then a living example of a human-sized coelacanth was discovered in 1938.

Modern crocodiles are living fossils — they closely resemble their ancestors who lived during the time of the dinosaurs.

41

"Hey! Didn't they find some human footprints together with dinosaur footprints?"

What a find that would be — like the Flintstones come to life! But rumors of human footprints and dinosaur tracks together are just that — rumors.

The last dinosaurs vanished from the Earth about 60 million years before the first humans appeared. That's a scientific estimate, but it isn't a guess. Over and over, scientists have confirmed that there was a huge time gap between dinosaurs and humans. They were never on the planet at the same time. So, how did fantastic claims of human-with-dinosaur tracks get started?

It all began with a flood in Texas in 1908. The deadly waters devastated the small town of Glen Rose — and also exposed rock that had been buried since the time of the dinosaurs. Not long after, a local teenager made an amazing discovery — huge three-toed footprints preserved in the rock. These tracks were made by a large dinosaur similar to *Tyrannosaurus rex* that walked upright on two legs. More than 100 million years earlier, this animal walked through some

Long ago, dinosaurs left behind footprints in what is now Texas.

muck. Its footprints were then covered with tons of mud and eventually became fossilized.

Locals soon realized that the area was crisscrossed by dinosaur tracks. Then, a few years later, another kid found tracks of a different shape. They looked a little bit like giant human footprints!

People began to chisel out the dinosaur tracks and "human" footprints to sell. This was extremely hard work. Cutting out the big tracks took so long that it was hardly worth the money. Then someone realized there was an easier way. Why not start with loose rocks and chisel in fake footprints? Sure, it was a bit dishonest, but …

One day, a paleontologist named Roland Bird came across the giant human footprints in a store. At first, they astounded him, but he soon figured out that the tracks were as fake as three-dollar bills. (They were too perfect, and their shape made no sense.)

But here's the silver lining. The local people Bird questioned led him to the real dinosaur tracks. Bird was amazed at the variety of tracks and gradually pieced together the story they told. Herds of huge four-legged dinosaurs had crossed a shallow mudflat. Two-legged, three-toed dinosaurs stalked them, and other kinds of dinosaurs lived with them along what was once an ancient shoreline. The tracks tell us things about how these dinosaurs moved and interacted that we could never have learned any other way.

The "human" footprints weren't human at all. Two-legged dinosaurs left footprints of various shapes, depending how they walked. We know this for a fact because there are trackways where one individual left footprints of two shapes. Walking upright, it left short birdlike tracks. When crouching, it left tracks with an elongated

"heel." Soft mud oozed back into the tracks and erased the three-clawed toes. When fossilized, this left big oblong shapes vaguely similar to giant human footprints. From there, imagination did the rest.

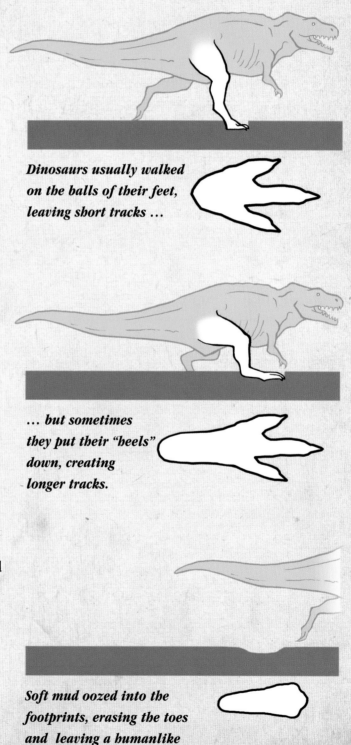

Dinosaurs usually walked on the balls of their feet, leaving short tracks …

… but sometimes they put their "heels" down, creating longer tracks.

Soft mud oozed into the footprints, erasing the toes and leaving a humanlike footprint.

"How could evolution produce something as complicated as my eyes?"

Yes, eyes are complicated. They have many parts that work together: an auto-focus lens, an iris to control the amount of light entering the eye, a bunch of little muscles to control the direction of our gaze and so on.

Some people argue that eyes could not work if any part were missing. For example, they say an eye without a lens couldn't focus. Therefore, eyes could not have evolved in small steps from simpler designs — they had to be made all at once. Goodbye, Darwin!

This might sound pretty convincing, except for one thing: It's just not true that eyes need all those parts to work. As Darwin pointed out, nature today is full of eye designs much simpler than ours.

For example, there are worms with clusters of light-sensitive cells on their skin. These cells let the worms tell night from day. Then there are animals such as flatworms with eyes that are simple dents lined with light-sensitive cells. These cells can detect the direction light comes from and even detect motion.

This sea creature, called a flatworm, has many simple cup-shaped eyes on its body.

Simple light sensitive cells ...

... lead to cup-shaped eyes ...

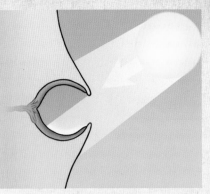

... that lead to pinhole eyes like those of the chambered nautilus.

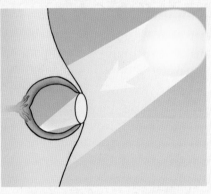

A transparent cover develops to protect the eye ...

... which leads to crude lenses ...

... and finally to high-quality lenses like ours.

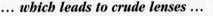

Some animals have deeper cup-shaped eyes that give them better vision, although it's still extremely blurry. But simply narrowing the opening of cup-shaped eyes fixes that problem. A narrow "pinhole" opening helps focus, even without a lens. (Some photographers use pinhole cameras that work in exactly this way.) In nature today, a squid relative called the chambered nautilus has this type of pinhole eye.

Then there are animals whose pinhole eyes are sealed over and protected by a bit of transparent skin. Any slight bulge in this transparent covering creates a crude lens that helps focus light. This happens in many animals today, including the apple snail. It's easy to see how top-quality lenses like ours could evolve — any improvement in the clarity or focusing power of the lens is a step in the right direction.

These many kinds of eyes illustrate the series of tiny steps that could slowly transform ordinary skin cells into complex human-type eyes. Every step works. Every step is an improvement. And every step is found in animals alive today.

The pinhole eyes of the chambered nautilus are just open hollow spaces with no covering lens.

"How could walking animals turn into flying animals? That seems like an awfully big jump!"

Not only have non-flying animals evolved into flying animals, but it seems that this happens quite often. Wing-flapping flight has evolved at least four separate times. Pterosaurs, birds, bats and insects are all examples of flying animals that independently evolved from walking or crawling ancestors.

This seems amazing. After all, either an animal can fly or it can't, right? Isn't that a big evolutionary leap to make more than once?

Not so fast! It's true that some animals can fly (such as eagles), while others can't fly at all (such as rhinoceroses). But those two extremes aren't the whole story.

People sometimes overlook the fact that many animals can sort of fly. These critters have the ability to parachute (fall slowly) or glide (steer and travel horizontally while falling).

This makes sense when you think about it. A lot of animals live in trees — and falling can be deadly. Think how you'd drop like a brick if you fell out of a tree. Then imagine what a big advantage it would be to have any degree of control over how far you could fall or jump.

Some animals, such as squirrels, make daring leaps from tree to tree many times a day. This is a risky business, so most squirrel-like mammals have evolved at least some ability to slow their falls by spreading out their bodies and parachuting down. In several animals, a further evolutionary leap

has occurred: They can glide gracefully through the air using skin flaps stretched between their legs. (American flying squirrels, Australian sugar gliders and the flying lemurs of the Philippines all evolved this ability independently of one another.)

Mammals aren't the only animals that glide from tree to tree. Some lizards use skin flaps along their sides to help them glide. Other lizards evolved ribs that can stretch out into gliding "wings." And some tree frogs use gigantic feet to help them glide.

Even more bizarre are the gliding snakes. They flatten their bodies, coil up and launch themselves out of trees in strange-looking but successful glides. There are even fish that glide. These "flying fish" use winglike fins to soar out of the water to escape predators, staying aloft for up to 45 seconds at a time. (Stare at a clock while it ticks off 45 seconds and you'll get a feeling for how astounding this is for a fish.)

Gliding has evolved many times in many groups of animals. The details are different, but the basic feat is common: Animals use their bodies to slow, control and extend the way they fall through the air.

By comparison, the Wright brothers' history-making first airplane flight was only 12 seconds long.

For most of human history, we've thought of flying as something almost like magic. Yet, flying and gliding are remarkably common in nature. It took advanced technology in the form of airplanes for humans to achieve this ancient dream, but evolution has given the gift of flight to creatures in many branches of the animal kingdom.

Scientists believe that many flying animals, such as this Archeopteryx evolved from tree-dwelling, gliding ancestors.

47

"Isn't the web of life too complex to have come about through evolution?

It would be hard to look at the natural world and not be impressed. Living things exist with other living things in complicated relationships that seem to work for all.

For example, the main food source for bees is nectar and pollen from flowers. When bees carry pollen from flower to flower, the plants use it to create seeds and reproduce. Bees and flowers need each other to survive.

Or look at what happens when a plant or animal dies. Every part of it is eaten by scavengers, broken down by bacteria, or absorbed into the soil where it will be used as food by trees and plants. Nothing goes to waste.

Some people think that nature is just too well organized and sophisticated to have got there through a series of small evolutionary changes. But here's a news flash: Natural processes aren't always so efficient. Some parts of nature are downright dumb and wasteful.

This earthworm is helping to break down organic matter so that it can be used by plants to help them grow.

49

Take trees, for example. "Why," asks biologist Richard Dawkins, "are trees in forests so tall?"

It might seem like a silly question, but a few hundred million years ago there were no tall trees anywhere on the planet. Why did forest trees evolve such long trunks? Why do their branches need to be so high off the ground?

"The short answer," Dawkins explains, "is that all the other trees are tall, so no one tree can afford not to be. It would be over-shadowed if it did." Trees need light to survive. To reach up to the sunlight, a tree needs to grow as tall as the neighboring trees.

Just imagine if trees didn't need to compete with their neighbors. They might be able to put their energy to better use, such as producing and spreading lots of seeds. More seeds would help ensure a tree's genes would be passed on to the next generation. Producing seeds takes valuable nutrients and energy. So does growing. In nature, everything is a trade-off. If a tree didn't have to grow such a long trunk, it would have far more resources to invest in seeds.

So, think about this: If all trees were just half their current height, they would all be much better off. All of the half-sized trees would get exactly the same amount of sunlight as they do now, but they wouldn't have to waste so much energy growing tall. Put that way, it's obvious: all trees should be short, if only they could all somehow "agree" to it. But that's not what happens in nature.

Why not? The problem is that plants and animals can't look at the big picture. In nature, everything just busily works for its own personal advantage on its own little piece of turf. Squirrels, trees, bacteria in the soil — all just grow and reproduce as best they can.

Trees are built simply to pass on their own genes to the next generation — even if doing this harms other trees. This leads to a race for the sky.

Imagine a forest where all trees happened to be short. The first tree to have a mutation for greater height would get extra sunlight, while its neighbors would get more shade. This would give the taller tree an edge in gathering energy, making seeds and passing on genes. So, in a short forest,

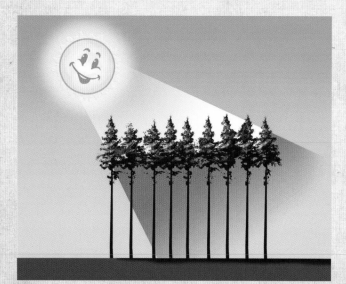

Trees are tall so they can reach the sunlight.

But they could all reach the sunlight at less cost if they were all short.

mutations for tallness will be passed on more frequently than genes for shortness.

In a forest that is already tall, it would be hard for a new mutation for shortness to take hold. A shortness mutation would be a disadvantage because short trees can't reach the sunlight as well, which means they would be unlikely to thrive and pass on their genes for shortness.

(It's like a concert where everyone starts off comfortably seated. At first, everyone can see just fine. But if a few people stand up to see better, they block the view for others. Soon everyone has to stand up for the same view they had in the first place — and no one can sit back down.)

The result is that every tree spends a huge proportion of its resources on growing tall, even though the whole forest would be better off if it were short. As Richard Dawkins says, "It seems so pointless, so wasteful."

But that's nature. Natural selection doesn't produce a perfect world. It produces a world in which all the billions of individual life-forms furiously compete to survive and reproduce. This vast, unimaginably complex

competition evens out to support impressively stable ecosystems. But natural selection also results in some tremendously wasteful relationships — and "ecological balance" is just what we call it when the competition between species grinds down to a long, long series of tie games.

Why not let the sunshine come to you?

But then, if some trees evolve to be taller, the others must keep up …

… and when all the trees are tall, shorter trees have a major disadvantage.

"People make it sound like evolution explains where life came from. Is that true? How did life get started in the first place?"

We know a tremendous amount about the way evolution shaped life on Earth once evolution began. But we do not know *how* life started.

The fossil record goes back almost to the dawn of simple microscopic life on Earth, billions of years ago, but eventually it fades out. One reason is that most of the rocks from the surface of early Earth have been recycled into the interior of the planet, taking many of the earliest fossils with them. (Volcanoes bring new rock to the surface, while old rocks are slowly forced back down by the movements of the Earth's crust.) This makes the question of the origin of life very hard to study.

But scientists are working on it. They've learned a lot about what early Earth was like. Many of the ingredients needed for life were present soon after the planet cooled from its molten birth: water, warmth, certain kinds of chemicals delivered by comets and so on. Scientists also know how the complex chemical components of life could form from simple ingredients. Finally, they now understand some of the possible processes that may have kick-started life.

Still, the origin of life remains one of the greatest puzzles in science. What an exciting and important question! Perhaps you'll be the one to solve it!

"What about religion?"

This is a question people often ask when wondering about evolution. They want to connect the discoveries of science to their religious understanding.

Unfortunately, this isn't something science can help with. Individual scientists may have personal opinions about religious matters, but science as a whole has nothing to say about religion.

Science is our most reliable method for sorting out how the natural world functions, but it can't tell us what those discoveries mean in a spiritual sense. Your family, friends and community leaders are the best people to ask about religious questions.

THE MAJESTIC POWER OF EVOLUTION

Though there are limits to evolution, its power is nonetheless awesome and majestic. The fact that such a process could generate the teeming diversity of the natural world is as stunning today as it was in Darwin's time.

"There is grandeur in this view of life," wrote Darwin. He marveled that "from so simple a beginning endless forms most beautiful and most wonderful have been, and are being, evolved."

Evolution has shaped and polished every facet of the living world: the flight of a hummingbird, the eyes of an eagle, the mimicry of a stick insect — even a brain like yours, clever enough to comprehend the workings of nature. Billions of species have existed on Earth — each precious, each amazing, each a jewel in the crown of the universe.

And here's the spine-tingling thing: You're related to every species, every person, every living thing that has ever existed on this planet. Every single one.

All creatures, from the lowliest bacteria to the blue whale, are branches that have evolved on the great tree of life!

Glossary

ancestors: all of the living things from which a living thing is descended — parents, grandparents, great-grandparents, great-great-grandparents and so on

convergent evolution: the tendency for living things to evolve similar features in response to similar challenges. For example, predator fish often evolved torpedo-shaped bodies that enabled them to swim fast while hunting prey.

diversity of life: the many different species of living things found in the natural world today and in the fossil record

DNA: the long, chain-like molecules that contain chemically coded instructions — called genes — for growing living things

evolution: the process of random mutation and natural selection through which living things change from generation to generation

fossils: bones or other parts of ancient living things that are preserved by turning into rock

fossil record: everything scientists have learned about the history of life on Earth by studying fossils

genes: the chemical instructions for growing a living thing

geology: the scientific study of the rocks that make up Earth's crust

hominids: modern humans and our closest extinct relatives, such as Neanderthals

ichthyosaurs: a group of extinct swimming reptiles with bodies that resembled sharks. Ichthyosaurs lived during the time of the dinosaurs.

mutations: random (unpredictable), permanent changes in the genetic instructions for growing a living thing

natural selection: the process through which advantageous genes are passed on to future generations. Living things born with natural advantages are more likely to survive and reproduce than those born with natural disadvantages.

offspring: living things that result from the reproduction of other living things — seeds, young or children

predators: animals that hunt other animals for food

prey: animals that are hunted as food by other animals

pterosaurs: a group of extinct, flying reptiles that lived during the time of the dinosaurs

reproduction: the process through which living things produce offspring

species: a group of living things that can reproduce with one another but not with other life-forms

survival of the fittest: the idea that living things born with natural advantages are more likely to survive and reproduce than those with natural disadvantages

traits: features or characteristics of living things. Traits come from the genetic instructions of a living thing and can be passed on to offspring.

transitional fossils: fossils that have characteristics showing they are related to two other species in the fossil record

Index